OREGON

wild and beautiful

Photography by Fred Pflughoft, David M. Morris and Charles A. Blakeslee

American and World Geographic Publishing / Montana Magazine

ISBN: 1-56037-154-4 (Mountain version)   ISBN: 1-56037-152-8 (Coast version)
Photography © 2000 Fred Pflughoft, David M. Morris, John L. Hinderman
and Charles A. Blakeslee
© 2000 American World Geographic Publishing

For more information on our books call or write:
American and World Geographic Publishing, P.O. Box 5630,
Helena, Montana, 59604, (406) 443-2842 or (800) 654-1105.
www.montanamagazine.com
merle_guy@lee.net
Printed in China

Above: Mount Hood and Trillium Lake. FRED PFLUGHOFT

Page one: Oxalis and sword ferns proliferate on Neahkahnie
Mountain. DAVID M. MORRIS

Leaves of false hellebore along the Metolius River.
FRED PFLUGHOFT

Anyone who has lived in or visited Oregon does not have superlatives to describe its scenic beauty. Even reference books simply describe it as one of our most beautiful states. I have traveled and photographed extensively in the western United States for most of my adult life, and Oregon still never ceases to amaze and surprise me with its variety. From its rugged, weathered Pacific Ocean coastline, to its majestic volcanic Cascades, and on to its vast high and dry Great Basin country, Oregon has a special place for everyone. Because of that, many photographers find themselves returning time and again to the same place and that is why it took four of us to capture the diversity of this state on theses pages.

For me, the Great Basin country became a personal photo safari. I remember vividly discovering how much this part of Oregon has to offer photographically. In spring of 1988, I visited Hart Mountain National Antelope Refuge for the first time. Hiking up tiny Rock Creek among huge aspens towering high into the deep azure sky, I became enthralled with the interplay of light. During more visits I saw that this least populated, and seldom visited, part of the state has some of the grandest landscapes anywhere. I hope you enjoy my vision of this unique part of Oregon.

For David, the coast has a special allure, and you will enjoy his special way of seeing its beauty. He has captured for us on film some of the best images you will see in print of this spectacular part of Oregon.

As for Chuck, he brings to this book his love of the Cascades and the Columbia Gorge. His work, too, gives us a different perspective on many scenes that have become familiar to those who know Oregon. Some of my favorite shots of the Oregon Cascades are images he has taken, and I only wish I had been there to enjoy the play of light on the landscape with him. I had the pleasure of photographing with him recently in Grand Teton National Park in Wyoming and his enthusiasm for his photography is contagious!

With his love of wildlife, John made a special contribution showing Oregon creatures.

I know I can speak for all of us when I say we hope you enjoy your journey through "Wild and Beautiful Oregon" and that it inspires you to new levels of enthusiasm for getting out and seeing all the spectacular beauty of this wonder-filled state.

From all of us,
Fred Pflughoft

Snow-covered trees on the Deschutes National Forest. FRED PFLUGHOFT

Facing page: A fence in Mann Lake cuts through the reflection of Steens Mountain. FRED PFLUGHOFT

Twilight tints downtown Portland and the Willamette River. CHARLES A. BLAKESLEE

Pond lilies in Sparks Lake, at the foot of Mount Bachelor. FRED PFLUGHOFT

An osprey lands a rainbow trout on the Grande Ronde River. JOHN L. HINDERMAN

Hay, rolled and stacked beneath Abert Rim, east of Fremont National Forest near the town of Valley Falls. FRED PFLUGHOFT

Above: Snow geese at Summer Lake Wildlife Area in Lake County. FRED PFLUGHOFT

Below: Coaxing a flame with flint and tinder at Fort Clatsop National Memorial, Astoria. FRED PFLUGHOFT

The roofs of Old Town Astoria and the Astoria Bridge. FRED PFLUGHOFT

Facing page: Starfish cling to a coastal rock on Short Sand Beach. DAVID M. MORRIS

Mist seeps into folds of the coast near Neskowin.   DAVID M. MORRIS

Above: Aspens in autumn at Hart Mountain National Antelope Refuge, northeast of Lakeview. FRED PFLUGHOFT

Right: A mule deer fawn angles for a drink of water. JOHN L. HINDERMAN

The petals of a wild iris retain a few beads of dew. DAVID M. MORRIS

Facing page: White on green. Wahkeena Falls in Columbia River Gorge National Scenic Area.
FRED PFLUGHOFT

Above: A patch of potential pie filling on Sauvie Island, down the river from Portland. CHARLES A. BLAKESLEE

Right: Artifacts, whitened and rusted, grace the side of a barn in Baker County. FRED PFLUGHOFT

Facing page: A brush of autumn colors at the water's edge, near McKenzie Pass in the Cascades. DAVID M. MORRIS

Wizard Island, a volcanic cone, keeps its
head above the deep waters of Crater
Lake in Crater Lake National Park.

FRED PFLUGHOFT

A burrowing owl, perching against a sky of purple and pink in eastern Oregon. JOHN L. HINDERMAN

Left: The tree line bows before, from left, South and Middle Sisters and Broken Top, in the Cascades. DAVID M. MORRIS

Mount Hood, the view from Timberline Lodge. FRED PFLUGHOFT

Facing page: Mount Washington makes a point above Meadow Lake. DAVID M. MORRIS

Above: Visitors and residents enjoy shopping on Bay Street in Florence's Old Town.
FRED PFLUGHOFT

Right: Rocks enjoy respite at Bandon Beach, south of Coos Bay. FRED PFLUGHOFT

Below: Fishing boats reflecting at Bandon. FRED PFLUGHOFT

Globe penstemon seems to sprout from granite in the Wallowa Mountains. DAVID M. MORRIS

Right: Sunset at Fish Lake, Rogue River National Forest. CHARLES A. BLAKESLEE

Ponderosa pines and fresh snow near the town of Sisters. DAVID M. MORRIS

Lava Butte, at 5,016 feet, in Newberry National Volcanic Monument. FRED PFLUGHOFT

Solitary bloom among oxalis leaves in Columbia Gorge. DAVID M. MORRIS

Facing page: Water runs a gauntlet of moss and rock, Rogue River Gorge. CHARLES A. BLAKESLEE

Mouths of many moods on the Deschutes River. FRED PFLUGHOFT

Facing page: Crooked River flows by Smith Rock, in Smith Rock State Park. FRED PFLUGHOFT

Sand dunes where the Siuslaw River meets the sea, Oregon Dunes National Recreation Area. FRED PFLUGHOFT

Facing page: Coquille River Lighthouse at Bandon. FRED PFLUGHOFT

Right: Weathered barn on the P Ranch, part of Malheur National Wildlife Refuge in Harney County. FRED PFLUGHOFT

Below: Dried mud in the Painted Hills, John Day Fossil Beds National Monument. FRED PFLUGHOFT

Wood, sculpted by wind, against backdrop of Three Sisters and, at right, Broken Top. DAVID M. MORRIS

Silver Falls State Park, east of Salem. CHARLES A. BLAKESLEE

Rhododendrons, blessed with a view of Mount Hood. CHARLES A. BLAKESLEE

Facing page: Climber hiking near Broken Top in Three Sisters Wilderness, Deschutes National Forest. FRED PFLUGHOFT

A lighthouse warns of a tumultuous shoreline at Cape Arago, near Coos Bay. DAVID M. MORRIS

Above: Excavation and construction site on the beach at Devil's Elbow State Park, near Heceta Head. FRED PFLUGHOFT

Right: Outdoor recreation and scenic views are features of Ashland's hundred-acre Lithia Park. CHARLES A. BLAKESLEE

45

Lupine at the feet of oak in Mayer State Park. CHARLES A. BLAKESLEE

Facing page: Full moon shines on Lost Lake, Mount Hood National Forest. CHARLES A. BLAKESLEE

Broken Top, *sans* snow, in *Three Sisters Wilderness*. FRED PFLUGHOFT

Ponderosa pines in Winema National Forest, north of Klamath Falls. FRED PFLUGHOFT

Right: Wind surfing on the Columbia River, in Celilo Park. FRED PFLUGHOFT

Below: Foxglove near Nehalem, on the coast. DAVID M. MORRIS

Translucent veils at Lower Proxy Falls, Willamette National Forest. FRED PFLUGHOFT

Sailboats and sunset on Waldo Lake, Willamette National Forest.
FRED PFLUGHOFT

53

Facing page: Bands of time—Painted Hills Unit of John Day Fossil Beds National Monument. FRED PFLUGHOFT

Still life by the wind—dried flowers and waves of sand at Alkali Lake. FRED PFLUGHOFT

Lupine forms a garland at the foot of Three Fingered Jack, Deschutes National Forest. CHARLES A. BLAKESLEE

The lights of Bend and a purple sky at sunset. DAVID M. MORRIS

Left: Salt Creek Falls, Willamette National Forest. CHARLES A. BLAKESLEE

Below: Forest Grove centers wine country; seen here is Laurel Ridge Winery. CHARLES A. BLAKESLEE

Facing page: Bear grass on shore of Scout Lake, beneath Mount Jefferson in the Cascades. DAVID M. MORRIS

Following pages: Alpenglow on South Sister and Camp Lake in the Three Sisters Wilderness, Willamette National Forest. FRED PFLUGHOFT

Right: Brothers in big hats at Sisters Rodeo. FRED PFLUGHOFT

Below: A typically Victorian embellishment graces the gable of a weathered barn at William L. Finley National Wildlife Refuge near Corvallis. FRED PFLUGHOFT

Facing page: Lupine and Indian paintbrush bloom near Russell Lake, below Mount Jefferson. DAVID M. MORRIS

Sun rays pierce the coastal fog that enshrouds a tree. DAVID M. MORRIS

The wreck of the Peter Iredale, Fort Stevens State Park at the mouth of the Columbia River. CHARLES A. BLAKESLEE

Upward mobility at Smith Rock State Park. FRED PFLUGHOFT

Facing page: Autumn along the Deschutes River, near Aspen Camp. DAVID M. MORRIS

Above: Youngsters provide local color at Fort Stevens State Park, north of Warrenton. FRED PFLUGHOFT

Right: Newberry Crater looms above Paulina Lake and resort boats. FRED PFLUGHOFT

Elowah Falls on McCord Creek, Columbia River Gorge National Scenic Area. CHARLES A. BLAKESLEE

Facing page: Crater Lake National Park takes its name from the waters that filled a basin left by the eruption and collapse of Mount Mazama, about 7,700 years ago. CHARLES A. BLAKESLEE

Following pages: Fanfare of purple and pink over South Sister, left center, Broken Top, at right, and Sparks Lake. CHARLES A. BLAKESLEE

Dry land and wetland at Malheur National Wildlife Refuge, from Buena Vista Overlook. FRED PFLUGHOFT

Facing page: A sign of the tides—the beach at Fort Stevens State Park. FRED PFLUGHOFT

A fence frames Mount McLoughlin near Four Mile Creek, Winema National Forest. CHARLES A. BLAKESLEE

Facing page: Cape Falcon, north of Manzanita. DAVID M. MORRIS

A cinnamon teal dabbles in Malheur National Wildlife Refuge.
JOHN L. HINDERMAN

Left: Paulina Peak and Paulina Lake, looking toward the Cascade Crest.
FRED PFLUGHOFT

Below: Elevator and silos near Grass Valley, southeast of The Dalles.
FRED PFLUGHOFT

Tulips are cultivated near Woodburn, south of Portland. CHARLES A. BLAKESLEE

Surf blasts through Arch Rock, at Samuel H. Boardman State Park. CHARLES A. BLAKESLEE

Catching the Sunrise Lift at Mount Bachelor. FRED PFLUGHOFT

Left: First light on the Three Sisters. FRED PFLUGHOFT

On an October day, ice begins to take hold of Big Lake and early snow dresses Mount Washington. CHARLES A. BLAKESLEE

An incoming fog threatens to obscure a patch of daisies and foxgloves near Cape Perpetua.
CHARLES A. BLAKESLEE

Facing page: The McKenzie River still rushes below Sahalie Falls in Willamette National Forest. FRED PFLUGHOFT

Balsamroot, desert parsley and prairie star in the Columbia River Gorge. DAVID M. MORRIS

Many trees have been disarmed by the winds swirling around North and Middle Sister in the Cascades. FRED PFLUGHOFT

After drying it, the sun casts a glow on the shore of Lake Abert in Lake County. FRED PFLUGHOFT

The suns last rays accent The Needles and Haystack Rock at Cannon Beach. CHARLES A. BLAKESLEE

In autumn, vine maple lends its reds to a golden undergrowth near Santiam Pass. FRED PFLUGHOFT

Mule ears and Indian paintbrush color Big Summit Prairie in the Ochoco Mountains.   DAVID M. MORRIS

A rainbow leads behind the curtain of Sahalie Falls on the McKenzie River, Willamette National Forest. CHARLES A. BLAKESLEE

Above: A wooden bridge spans the Japanese Garden in Portland's Washington Park.   CHARLES A. BLAKESLEE

Left: A mouth-watering bunch of Cabernet Sauvignon grapes west of Roseburg.   CHARLES A. BLAKESLEE

Lilies on Hosmer Lake, along Cascade Lakes Highway and under the eyes of South Sister and Broken Top. FRED PFLUGHOFT

Sea anemone and starfish above a tidal pool along the central coast. CHARLES A. BLAKESLEE

Facing page: Tinted sky and raging surf at Seal Rock, south of Newport. DAVID M. MORRIS

Left: Skiing Hayden Glacier in the Three Sisters Wilderness. FRED PFLUGHOFT

Below: Warner Peak rises above Hart Mountain National Antelope Refuge. FRED PFLUGHOFT

Facing page: Wildflowers carpet the rolling meadows below Mount Hood. CHARLES A. BLAKESLEE

Above: A burst of fall maple on Sunset Summit, in the Coast Range. CHARLES A. BLAKESLEE

Right: A covered bridge at Harris, west of Corvallis. CHARLES A. BLAKESLEE

Facing page: Spring runoff at Horsetail Falls in the Columbia River Gorge National Scenic Area. FRED PFLUGHOFT

Following pages: Sunset at Heceta Head, Devil's Elbow State Park. FRED PFLUGHOFT

Dark clouds and sun rays seem to do battle at sunrise over the Columbia River. JOHN L. HINDERMAN

Left: Meadow of lupine and balsamroot at the Tom McCall Preserve, on the bluffs above the Columbia River at Rowena. CHARLES A. BLAKESLEE

Above: The Dalles Dam impedes the Columbia at The Dalles. FRED PFLUGHOFT

Below: A sere January landscape in the Sheepshead Mountains in Malheur County. FRED PFLUGHOFT

Facing page: Waves crest among sea stacks at Ecola State Park, just north of Cannon Beach.
CHARLES A. BLAKESLEE

Mists encircle a snowy Mount Bachelor, Deschutes National Forest. FRED PFLUGHOFT

Above: The wagons are circled at the Oregon Trail Interpretive Center on Flagstaff Hill, north of Baker City.
FRED PFLUGHOFT

Below: Winter dries cattails and ices Summer Lake, with Winter Ridge dusted in snow. FRED PFLUGHOFT

Above: Luminous vine maple in Willamette National Forest.
FRED PFLUGHOFT

Right: An immature short-eared owl. JOHN L. HINDERMAN

Facing page: An imposing escarpment below Eagle Cap
Mountain, overlooking Mirror Lake, in the Wallowa
Mountains. DAVID M. MORRIS

Rocks worn by the seas, Oswald West State Park in Manzanita. DAVID M. MORRIS

Facing page: Wave sculpture at Cape Arago, near Coos Bay. DAVID M. MORRIS

Sunrise on Broken Top in the Three Sisters Wilderness, Deschutes National Forest. DAVID M. MORRIS

Lupine on the shore of Wallowa Lake, near Joseph. DAVID M. MORRIS

Above: A fallen tree forms a natural bridge atop Whitehorse Falls in Umpqua National Forest. FRED PFLUGHOFT

Left: Leaves of false hellebore at the feet of aspens, Steens Mountain in Harney County. FRED PFLUGHOFT

Facing page: Fireweed and the lighthouse at Yaquina Head, north of Newport. CHARLES A. BLAKESLEE

Following pages: A surfer calls it a day at Short Sand Beach, Oswald West State Park in Manzanita. DAVID M. MORRIS

Lewis's monkeyflower, Indian paintbrush and arrowhead butterweed crowd a stream in the Cascades.   DAVID M. MORRIS